The Blessing
of
Feelings

Erika Nilsen and
Mary Ylvisaker Nilsen

Library of Congress Control Number: 2006934785

ISBN 978-0-9627147-4-0

Published in the United States by

Zion Publishing
1500 Crown Colony Court #540
Des Moines, Iowa 50315

www.zionpublishing.org

1-800-996-2777

Printed in China

Dear Readers,

Feelings are a gift—a deeply important part of who we are as human beings. They are neither good nor bad, right nor wrong. They are simply the body's response to what is happening both outside of us and within us. These emotions allow us to experience the fullness of life.

My mother Mary and I created this book as a tool for parents, grandparents and others to help the children they love understand and appreciate the blessing of feelings. Let the children learn the names of emotions and study the faces, so they can name their own feelings. Then talk about situations that bring up such feelings and times when they might have had a similar feeling. Assure them that a feeling is never wrong. It just is.

As a mother of three, I know all too well the crazy ups and downs of children's feelings. I also know how challenging it can be to help a child name his or her feeling and work through it in a healthy way. I sometimes want to tell my kids how they are feeling or even how they *should* feel. But that is not for me to do. The task of all parents and people who care for children is to allow them to feel what they feel, name it, and make healthy, constructive choices for moving through that feeling.

If you notice that a child seems unable to move beyond a feeling, particularly one of anger, sadness, shame, fear, or guilt, consult a professional for guidance on how to help him or her.

I hope and pray that the children you love will grow up knowing they are blessed by all those wonderful and strange feelings that come and go.

Erika Nilsen

Feelings come and feelings go.

You're blest because God made you so.

A feeling rises up to say

that something's wrong or you're OK.

On these pages we will show

feelings that both come and go.

Our faces in this book display

some ways that you might feel each day.

I'm sad . . .

I'm sad . . .

I'm sad
and blue.

I'm mad!

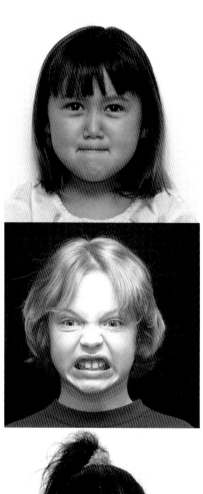

I'm mad!

I'm mad too!

I'm glad!

I'm glad!

I'm glad all
through!

What feeling is
inside of you?

Carl, Carl!
   Are you all right today?

I feel Cranky when I'm hungry . . .

but Content when all's OK.

Susie, Susie!
   Is there something wrong?

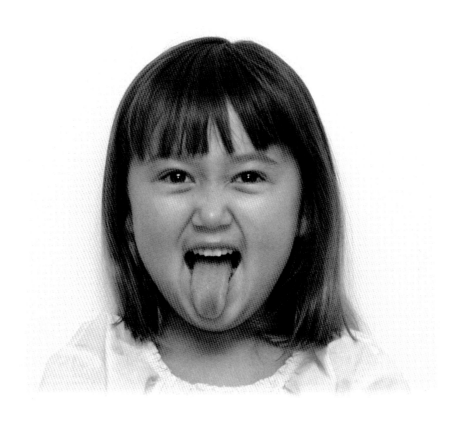

I like feeling Sassy . . .

and I love feeling Strong.

Henry, Henry!
   Are you finding ways to cope?

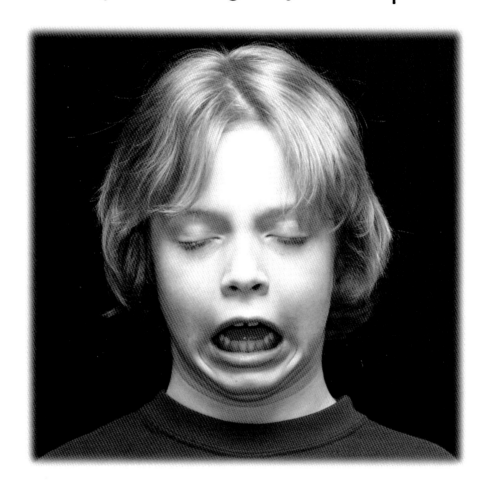

First I felt so Horrified . . .

but now I'm full of Hope.

Trisha, Trisha!
    You look a bit weary.

Are you Tired? Do you need a nap . . .

or are you just a little Teary?

Luke, Luke!
   Are you feeling all right?

I'm Livid 'cause we could have won . . .

but I'll be Loving by tonight.

Calvin, Calvin!
   What's up, dude?

Right now I'm feeling Carefree . . .

but I was Concerned and Confused.

Anna, Anna!
  What's happening inside of you?

I told a lie and feel Ashamed . . .

but I'm Afraid to tell the truth.

Freddie, Freddie!
   Are you OK with the plan?

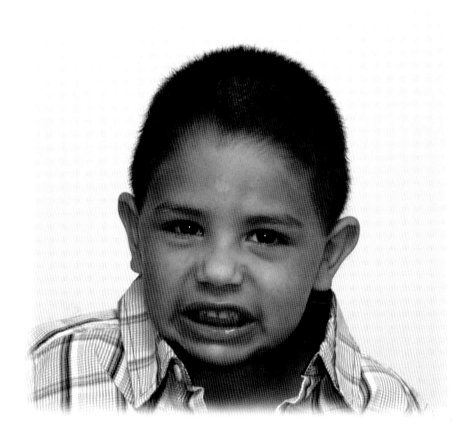

I'll feel Frustrated if we can't go . . .

but Fantastic if we can.

Sarah, Sarah!
How are you feeling inside?

Sometimes I'm feeling Silly . . .

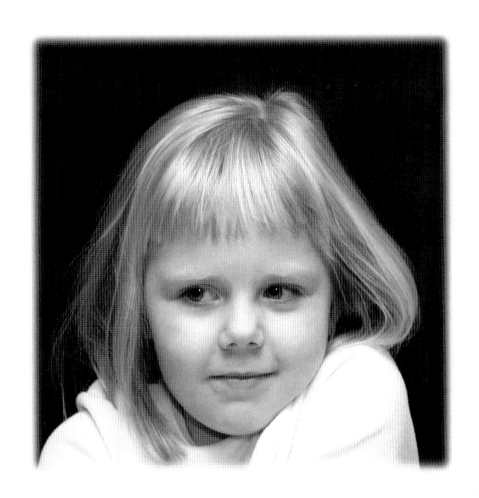

sometimes a little Shy.

Andrew, Andrew!
   How's your puppy today?

I'm Annoyed when he bites me . . .

but Amused when we play.

Julia, Julia!
　　What's the trouble all about?

I'm Joyful when they play with me . . .

but Jealous when they leave me out.

Bella, Bella!
   When is life at its best?

It's not when I am feeling Bummed . . .

but when I'm feeling Blest!

Try to guess
how these kids
are feeling now.

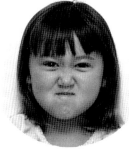